Look Inside an Electric Car

How It Works

Taylor Fenmore

Lerner Publications • Minneapolis

Lerner Publications Company
An imprint of Lerner Publishing Group, Inc.
241 First Avenue North
Minneapolis, MN 55401 USA

For reading levels and more information, look up this title at www.lernerbooks.com.

Main body text set in Billy Infant Regular. Typeface provided by SparkType.

Library of Congress Cataloging-in-Publication Data

Names: Fenmore, Taylor, author.
Title: Look inside an electric car : how it works / Taylor Fenmore.
Description: Minneapolis : Lerner Publications, [2024] | Series: Lightning bolt books. Under the hood | Includes bibliographical references and index. | Audience: Ages 6–9 | Audience: Grades 2-3 | Summary: "Electric cars take us to work and school, carry our packages, and race down highways without leaving pollution. Readers will enjoy carefully leveled text that explores the science behind these high-interest vehicles"— Provided by publisher.
Identifiers: LCCN 2023012378 (print) | LCCN 2023012379 (ebook) | ISBN 9798765608371 (lib. bdg.) | ISBN 9798765624425 (pbk.) | ISBN 9798765615867 (epub)
Subjects: LCSH: Electric automobiles—Juvenile literature. | BISAC: JUVENILE NONFICTION / Transportation / Cars & Trucks
Classification: LCC TL220 .F465 2024 (print) | LCC TL220 (ebook) | DDC 629.22/93—dc23/eng/20230322

LC record available at https://lccn.loc.gov/2023012378
LC ebook record available at https://lccn.loc.gov/2023012379

Manufactured in the United States of America
1-1009469-51491-4/28/2023

Table of Contents

Ready to Drive

An electric car zips down the road. Its motor is quiet. Its batteries are charged with electricity.

Electric cars are a type of vehicle. They run on electricity. People drive them many places including in towns and on highways.

Electric cars come in many styles.

Many Electric Cars

Electric cars can be better for the environment than cars that use gasoline. Burning gasoline creates gases that cause air pollution. Most electric cars don't create these gases.

Many cities use electric buses to move people around.

Some people drive electric cars or ride electric buses to work, school, or the store. Other people drive electric semitrucks to carry goods long distances.

Many electric cars only have an electric motor. The motor gets all its power from a battery.

Electric car engines can be much smaller than gasoline engines.

Some electric cars are hybrids. Hybrid electric cars have an electric motor and a gasoline engine. They use engines when they need extra power.

Hybrid cars use less gasoline than gasoline-powered cars.

Make it Move

To make an electric car move, the motor needs electricity. Electricity can be made from sunlight with solar panels.

Some homes have places to charge electric cars.

The car's charging port collects most of the energy from a charging station or an outlet at home.

Charging stations can be built in parking lots, letting people shop while their car charges.

People plug special chargers into the charging port to charge the car's battery. Some cities have public charging stations where many cars can be charged at once.

It takes about eight hours to fully charge an electric car. Most can go about 200 to 300 miles (322 to 483 km) on one charge.

There are over 130,000 public electric car chargers across the US.

Drivers press the brake pedal to stop the wheels. Another pedal tells the motor to move the wheels. The steering wheel moves the wheels left or right.

Some electric cars can drive over 200 miles (322 km) on a single charge.

The gearshift tells the transmission gears to shift between drive and reverse.

A driver uses a gearshift to let the wheels move forward or backward.

Parts of an Electric Car

Electric cars have two batteries. One battery powers the motor.

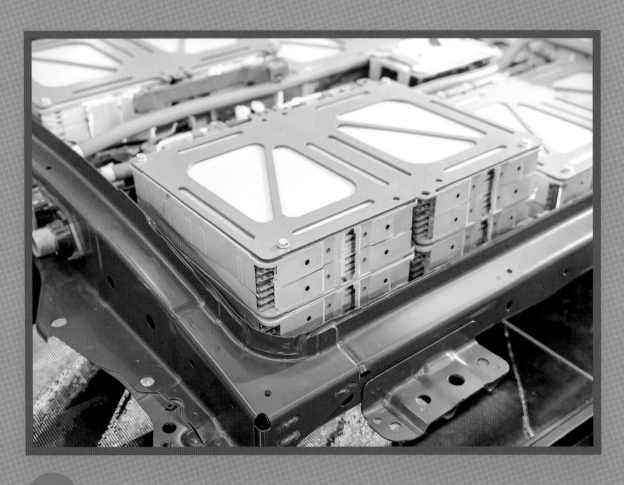

Many electric cars don't have ignition keys. Instead, drivers push a button to start the car.

The second battery helps turn the car on. It also helps run other systems such as the radio.

Electric cars have a system near the motor to help keep it cool. The two most common systems use fans or special liquids to cool the motor.

Many electric cars warm up faster in cold weather than gasoline cars.

More people are starting to drive electric cars. New electric cars will keep hitting the road every day.

Buyers can choose from many shapes and sizes of electric cars.

Electric Car Diagram

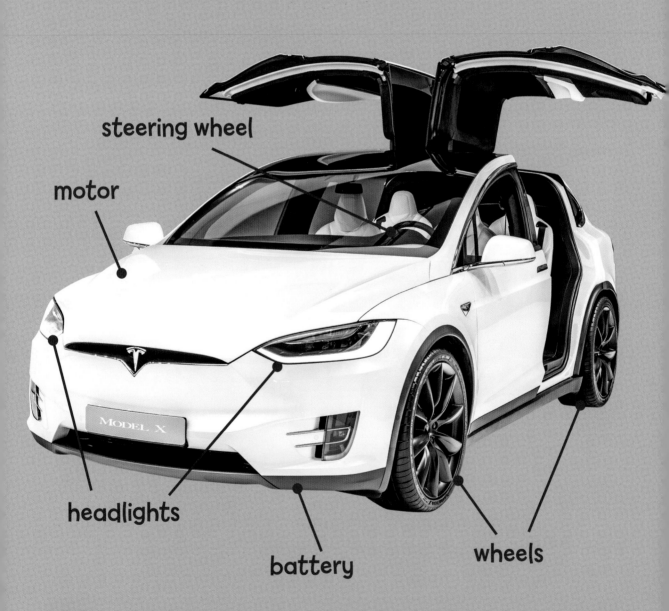

steering wheel

motor

headlights

battery

wheels

No Exhaust Pipes

Most cars need gasoline to run their engines. The engine burns gasoline to create heat for power. But burning gasoline creates gases. They exit the car through an exhaust pipe in the back. Too much exhaust creates air pollution. It can make people sick, affect climate change, and even make the sky less clear. Cars that run on only electricity do not have exhaust pipes because they do not create any exhaust.

Glossary

battery: an electric cell or group of cells that has an electric current to turn something on or give it power

charger: a device that gives power to batteries

engine: a machine that changes energy, such as heat from burning gasoline, into motion

gasoline: a type of liquid fuel. Many people call it gas even though it is a liquid.

gearshift: a part of a car that lets the driver change gears

hybrid: something, such as a car, that has two types of systems that can power it

motor: a machine that makes something move

port: an opening (as in a machine) for gas, steam, water, or energy to go in or out

vehicle: a machine used to transport people or goods

Learn More

Alliant Energy: Electric Vehicles (EVs)
https://www.alliantenergykids.com
/innovationsinenergy/electricvehicles

Kawa, Katie. *20 Fun Facts about Electricity*.
Buffalo: Gareth Stevens, 2024.

Kiddle: Electric Vehicles Facts for Kids
https://kids.kiddle.co/Electric_vehicle

Leed, Percy. *Look Inside a Big Rig: How It Works*.
Minneapolis: Lerner Publications, 2024.

Time for Kids: An Electric Future
https://www.timeforkids.com/g56/an-electric
-future-2/?rl=en-810

Vilardi, Debbie. *Electric Cars*. Minneapolis: Cody
Koala, 2019.

Index

Photo Acknowledgments

Image credits: Abu hasim.A/Shutterstock, p. 4; ginger_polina_bublik/Shutterstock, p .5; canadianPhotographer56/Shutterstock, p. 6; alexfan32/Shutterstock, p. 7; mujjjoa79/ Shutterstock, p. 8; Robert Bodnar T/Shutterstock, p. 9; seksan Mongkhonkhamsao/Getty Images, p. 10; Maskot/Getty Images, pp. 11, 13; somkanae sawatdinak/Shutterstock, p. 12; Zviahintsev Denis/Shutterstock, p. 14; Bilalstock/Shutterstock, p. 15; asharkyu/ Shutterstock, p. 16; Israel Sebastian/Getty Images, p. 17; Olexandr Panchenko/Shutterstock, p. 18; humphery/Shutterstock, p. 19; Grzegorz Czapski/Shutterstock, p. 20.

Cover: Photosite/Shutterstock.